Let's Investigate Plants!

Some Plants Eat Meat!

By Ruth Owen

KidHaven PUBLISHING

Published in 2024 by
KidHaven Publishing, an Imprint of Greenhaven Publishing, LLC
2544 Clinton St., Buffalo, NY 14224

Portions of this work were originally authored by Ruth Owen and published as *How Do Meat-Eating Plants Catch Their Food?*
All new material this edition authored by Ruth Owen.

Produced for Rosen by Ruby Tuesday Books Ltd
Editor for Ruby Tuesday Books Ltd: Mark J. Sachner
US Editor: Designer: Emma Randall

Photo Credits:
Cover, 1, 4–5, 6–7, 8–9, 10–11, 12–13, 14–15, 16, 18, 22–23, 24–25, 26, 27 (bottom), 29 © Shutterstock; 17, 20 © FLPA; 19 © Noah Elhardt; 21 © Chien Lee; 27 (top) © Petr Dlouhy.

Cataloging-in-Publication Data

Names: Owen, Ruth.
Title: Some plants eat meat! / Ruth Owen.
Description: Buffalo, New York : KidHaven Publishing, 2024. | Series: Let's investigate plants! | Includes glossary and index.
Identifiers: ISBN 9781534545571 (pbk.) | ISBN 9781534545588 (library bound) | ISBN 9781534545595 (ebook)
Subjects: LCSH: Carnivorous plants--Juvenile literature.
Classification: LCC QK917.O94 2024 | DDC 581.6--dc23

Manufactured in the United States of America

CPSIA compliance information: Batch #CSKH24: For further information contact Greenhaven Publishing LLC at 1-844-317-7404.

Contents

Little Carnivores

If you think of a meat eater, you might imagine a creature that can chase and attack, such as a big cat with sharp teeth and claws. However, some meat eaters cannot run, jump, or pounce on their prey.

These **carnivorous** living things must use a different set of tactics to catch their food. These meat eaters use traps, tricks, and even glue to capture their prey. Once caught, however, the victim's end is the same. All the struggling creature

can do is give in and wait to become the meal of a carnivorous plant. Around the world, there are many different **species** of meat-eating plants. Why do some plants capture animals as food—and how do they do it?

a fly being eaten by a Venus flytrap plant

How Do Plants Get Food?

Just like you, a plant needs food to give it the energy to live and grow. It also needs to take in extra nutrients.

Most plants, including meat eaters, make the food they need for energy from water, **carbon dioxide**, and sunlight. This process is called **photosynthesis**, and it takes place in the plant's leaves.

Plants big and small use sunlight, carbon dioxide, and water to make food.

A plant takes in water from the soil with its **roots**. The water is then delivered through the plant's stems to its leaves. The leaves take in carbon dioxide from the air through **microscopic** holes called **stomata**. Then, inside the plant's leaves, a substance called **chlorophyll** traps the energy in sunlight and uses it to turn the water and carbon dioxide into a sugary food. All plants use this type of food for energy.

Carnivorous plants make the food they need for energy through photosynthesis.

How Do Plants Get Nutrients?

The process of photosynthesis gives plants the sugary food they need for energy, but to be completely healthy, a plant also needs nutrients.

Nutrients are essential to help plants grow and produce leaves, flowers, and seeds. Nutrients such as nitrogen, potassium, calcium, and magnesium can be found dissolved in water in the soil. Most plants take in these nutrients through their roots when they take in water.

These garden plants are growing in soil containing plenty of nutrients.

Some plants, however, live in **habitats**, such as **bogs** or rocky places, where there is not much soil or where the soil contains few nutrients. These plants have developed an alternative way to obtain the nutrients they need. They get them from the bodies of animals!

a Venus flytrap growing in a rocky habitat

carnivorous pitcher plants growing in a boggy habitat

A Clever Trap

A Venus flytrap is a carnivorous plant with leaves that act as deadly traps for catching prey.

To attract their prey, the traps produce a sweet liquid called nectar. Flies and other insects land on the traps to feed on the **nectar**. Inside the traps, there are tiny trigger hairs. When an insect touches these hairs, the trap is triggered and snaps shut! The more the plant's victim struggles, the tighter the trap closes.

The traps on a Venus flytrap are edged with toothlike projections called cilia. These projections lace together to ensure that the trap stays tightly shut.

Venus flytraps grow in boggy habitats. They only grow wild in a few small areas on the east coast of the United States.

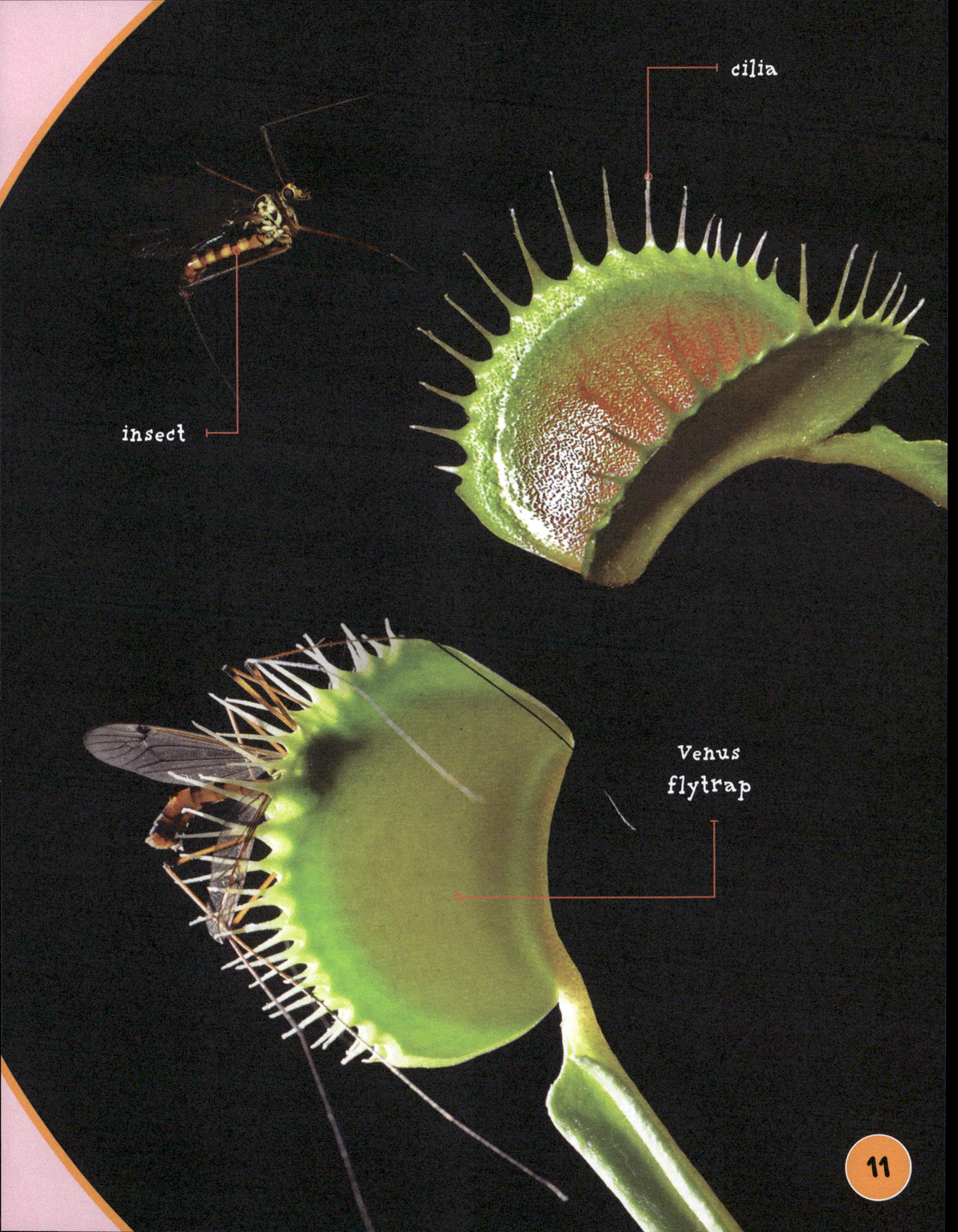
cilia
insect
Venus
flytrap

A Venus Flytrap's Meal

Once the trap on a Venus flytrap has closed around an insect, it is doomed!

The cilia on this trap are holding it tightly closed.

Now the trap's role changes. In fact, it becomes a lot like a tiny stomach. Juices begin to ooze from the trap. These juices act like the digestive juices that break down food in your stomach. Over several days, the juices from the trap dissolve the soft parts of the insect, turning them into a soft, soupy mass. Then the trap absorbs nutrients, such as nitrogen, from this mass.

After about 12 days, all that remains of the insect is its hard **exoskeleton**. The trap reopens and the dried-up husk of the insect is blown away by the wind or washed from the trap the next time it rains.

Death by Drowning

There are some meat-eating plants that kill their prey by drowning them!

There are many different species of carnivorous **pitcher** plants. They come in lots of shapes and sizes, but they all have a cup or tubelike part called a pitcher. The plant lures its prey with a meal of sweet nectar. However, inside the pitcher is a deadly pool of watery liquid where the hungry victims drown.

The liquid inside a pitcher contains juices that dissolve any soft, fleshy parts of an animal, releasing nutrients into the liquid. Then the pitcher absorbs the nutrients from the liquid. Finally, all that remains of the pitcher plant's victim is its dry, empty exoskeleton!

Cuplike pitchers dangle from the plant on a thin tendril.

Slipping and Sliding

North American pitcher plants are meat eaters that attract insects to the rims, or edges, of their tubelike pitchers with nectar. The pitchers' rims are dangerously slippery.

When an insect lands on a pitcher's rim, it starts to feed, but it may soon lose its footing. Then it will plunge into the liquid at the base of the pitcher. If the wet, panicked creature tries to climb out of the pitcher, it finds there is no escape. The inside walls of the pitcher are very slippery and contain downward-pointing hairs that make climbing upward nearly impossible. All the plant's victim can do is wait to be digested!

North American pitcher plants grow in bogs and other places where the ground is very wet.

North American pitcher plants

rim
downward-pointing hairs
ant feeding on nectar
liquid in pitcher
drowned ant

The Cobra Lilies

California pitcher plants are nicknamed cobra lilies because they are shaped like a rearing cobra snake. The plants even have a snakelike, leafy forked tongue!

These carnivorous plants have a range of horrifying tricks to trap and kill their prey. Insects enter the plant's bubble-like hoods to feed on nectar. The inside surface of the hood is slippery, so the insect may slip and fall down into the pitcher.

If an insect avoids slipping, it might try to escape, but even this is impossible. The many see-through patches in the hood look like escape holes, but they are not. The trapped insect crawls from patch to patch looking for a way out. Finally, the exhausted insect falls into the pitcher and drowns.

California pitcher plant
bubble-like hood
see-through patches
Leaves

The Rat Catchers

Some very large pitcher plants capture prey that's much bigger than flies or other insects.

Like other pitcher plants, the main prey of giant pitchers is insects. Sometimes, however, larger animals such as rats, shrews, and lizards may fall into the pitchers. Unable to escape from the slippery cups, these creatures then die and become food for the plants.

One of the largest species ever discovered was found on a mountainside in the Philippines. A British explorer and scientist, Stewart McPherson, discovered the plant in 2007. The largest of the plant's pitchers were 11 inches (28 cm) long and could hold just over 3 pints (1.5 L) of liquid. Stewart called the new species *Nepenthes attenboroughii*, naming it after a famous British **naturalist**, Sir David Attenborough.

a pitcher of
Nepenthes attenboroughii

a *rat* feeding on nectar from a giant pitcher plant species

Get Your Sweet Meal Here!

Some carnivorous plants use traps or liquid-filled pitchers to catch their prey. Pretty sundew plants catch their food using glue!

Sundews are carnivorous plants that grow in wet, boggy places almost everywhere around the world, except for the Arctic and Antarctica. There are about 160 different species of these plants.

Sundews are often just a few inches tall, so a person would need to look closely to see their amazing methods of trapping prey. The leaves of sundews are covered with tiny stalklike **glands** that produce a sticky glue. Each stalk has a glistening blob of glue on its end that smells like nectar. As an insect flies by the plant, it sees and smells the fake nectar and zooms in.

stalks
trapped fly
sundew plant leaf

Trapped in Glue!

Once the insect lands on the sundew's leaf looking for nectar, one leg gets stuck, then another.

The insect might beat its wings to aid its escape, only to find that they also touch the blobs of glue and become stuck. As the insect struggles to escape, the leaf curls around its prey. Then, with the insect still fighting for its life, the leaf releases juices that start to dissolve the creature.

As the insect's body breaks down, the leaf absorbs nutrients from its meal. Once the leaf has absorbed all the nutrients it can, it uncurls, leaving just the dried-up shell of its victim.

a sundew leaf curling around a trapped insect

This plant's pretty name comes from its deadly glue that glistens in sunlight and looks like dew.

Tiny but Deadly

A butterwort is a tiny but deadly plant with leaves that look as if they are covered with little drops of water or delicious nectar.

However, the shiny drops on the plant's leaves are drops of glue produced by tiny hairs. Once an insect gets trapped in the glue, the leaf produces juices that turn the insect into a soupy mass so its nutrients can be absorbed by the leaf.

It's hard to imagine that plants can actually be hunters, but it's true. If you're an insect, these living things are as deadly as a lion or a shark. Carnivorous plants may have leaves instead of claws and teeth, but with their traps, tricks, and glue, these little meat eaters are deadly killers!

a butterwort plant

This close-up view of a butterwort leaf shows the tiny hairs that produce glue for trapping prey.

Let's Investigate a Venus Flytrap

To catch its meal, a Venus flytrap must snap its leafy trap shut at exactly the right moment. If it makes its deadly move too soon, the insect might not be fully inside and will realize it's in danger. If the plant waits too long, its prey might fly away and escape.

If the plant closes its trap on an object that is not an insect, it will waste valuable energy. Also, each trap can only snap shut three or four times before it loses its effectiveness. So each trap is precious and the plant can't afford to wear out its traps capturing objects, such as a piece of dead leaf, that land on the trap by accident.

A Venus flytrap's timing has to be just right, so let's investigate how it works in this activity.

You can buy Venus flytraps from many garden centers that sell plants. You can also order them online. If you are lucky enough to see these plants growing wild where you live, DO NOT remove them from their natural habitat.

YOU WILL NEED:

- **a Venus flytrap plant**
- **a magnifying glass**
- **a pencil**
- **a watch (for timing seconds)**
- **a notebook and pen**

Step 1:
Begin by taking a close-up look at the plant's traps through the magnifying glass.
Do you see the hairs inside the traps?

Does each trap have the same number of hairs?

Step 2:
Draw the following table in your notebook.

ACTION	TRAP 1 DID THE TRAP CLOSE?	TRAP 2 DID THE TRAP CLOSE?
Touch the cilia		
Touch one hair (inside the trap) one time		
Touch one hair two times (within 1 second)		
Touch one hair two times (with a 5-second interval)		
Touch one hair two times (with a 10-second interval)		
Touch one hair two times (with a 30-second interval)		

Step 3:
Now investigate how the traps operate. Test one of the traps by carrying out the actions described in the table. Use the point of a pencil to gently touch the trap. Record your results in the table.

Step 4:
Now try again using a different trap and record your results.

Why? How? What?
When did the traps shut?
Why do you think the traps shut when they did and not at the other times?
(See page 32 for the answer.)

Glossary

bogs (BOGZ) Natural habitats where the ground is soft and very wet, and where lots of moss may grow. Bogs are usually part of a wetland.

carbon dioxide (KAHR-bun dy-OK-syd) A colorless gas in the air that plants use to make food. When humans and other animals breathe out, they release carbon dioxide into the air.

carnivorous (kahr-NIH-vuh-rus) Referring to an animal or plant that eats, or obtains nutrients from, meat.

chlorophyll (KLOR-uh-fil) The substance that gives plants their green color. Leaves use chlorophyll for making food during photosynthesis.

exoskeleton (EK-soh-skeh-leh-tun) The skeleton of animals such as insects and spiders that is on the outside of the body.

glands (GLANDZ) Organs that produce chemical substances in a plant or in an animal's body.

habitats (HA-buh-tats) Places where animals or plants normally live. A habitat may be a backyard, a forest, the ocean, or a mountainside.

microscopic (my-kreh-SKAH-pik) So small that an object can only be seen through a microscope and not with a person's eyes alone.

naturalist (NA-chuh-ruh-list) An expert in natural history, often a scientist, who studies plants, animals, and natural habitats.

nectar (NEK-tur) A sweet liquid produced by flowers that many insects and other animals eat.

nutrients (NOO-tree-ents) Substances needed by a plant or animal to help it live and grow. Most plants take in nutrients from the soil using their roots. Carnivorous plants obtain nutrients from the bodies of animals.

photosynthesis (foh-toh-SIN-thuh-sus) The process by which plants make food in their leaves using water, carbon dioxide, and sunlight.

pitcher (PIH-cher) A tube or cup-shaped part of a carnivorous plant that contains a liquid that drowns and then dissolves the plant's prey.

prey (PRAY) An animal that is hunted by other animals for food.

roots (ROOTS) Parts of plants that usually grow underground and are used by the plant for taking in water and nutrients from the soil. Roots also hold a plant steady in soil so it doesn't fall over.

species (SPEE-sheez) One type of living thing. The members of a species look alike and can reproduce together.

stomata (STOH-mah-tuh) Microscopic holes on a leaf that a plant uses for taking in carbon dioxide and releasing oxygen.

Websites

https://www.nwf.org/Educational-Resources/Wildlife-Guide/Plants-and-Fungi/Venus-Flytrap

https://www.carnivorousplants.org/cp/carnivory/what

https://www.nhm.ac.uk/discover/carnivorous-plants-meat-eaters-of-the-plant-world.html

Read More

Allan, John. *Plants (Amazing Life Cycles)*. Minneapolis, MN: Hungry Tomato Ltd., 2019.

Griffin, Mary. *Meat-Eating Venus Flytraps (Fantastic Plants)*. New York, NY: Rosen Publishing, 2023.

Nickel, Scott. *World's Grossest Plants (UpDog Books)*. Minneapolis, MN: Lerner Publishing Group, 2022.

Index

Answers

Pages 28-29

The traps on your plant probably shut when you touched a hair inside them twice with an interval of around five to ten seconds. Just one touch on a hair did not trigger a trap because it might be an object, such as a piece of debris, falling into the trap by accident. Two touches close together, however, recreated the movement of an insect walking around inside the trap, so the trap closed.